contents

welcome

Practical, creative, stress-reducing, and gratifying—sewing is many things to many people. If you've never sewn a stitch or your sewing skills need some fine-tuning, you'll be surprised at how easy it is to create personalized, fun projects for you and your home.

Inside this book, we'll acquaint you with the basic tools and essential techniques for successful sewing. Then, when you're comfortable with the basics, choose your favorite projects from our collection of quick-and-easy projects that will have you proudly saying, "I made it myself!"

The Staff

essential sewing box tools

Whether you're a first-time sewer or rediscovering the benefits of home sewing, the right tools will make your sewing experience successful and enjoyable. These six essentials will help each project go smoothly.

1. scissors

Scissors are available in a variety of sizes and styles. Choose a quality pair of large scissors for cutting fabrics and a small pair with sharp points for trimming threads and cutting precise shapes. Spring-loaded styles ease hand strain when cutting large fabric pieces, and cushioned grips add comfort. To prolong blade sharpness, use these scissors only for cutting fabrics and threads, not for cutting paper or performing other household tasks.

2. straight pins

Hold fabric pieces and trims in place as you cut or sew by using straight pins. Select from a variety of pins including those with glass heads, which hold up to heat, and plastic heads, which do not. Quilting pins are longer and thicker than standard straight pins, making them a good choice for holding bulky fabrics or multiple layers. When machine-stitching, avoid sewing over pins, which could cause your needle to break. Corral loose pins with a classic stuffed pincushion or a magnetic pin holder.

3. measuring tools

The measuring tape is the most basic of measuring tools. Its flexible nature is useful for measuring curved shapes, such as the circumference of an ottoman or the perimeter of an arched window. Other measuring tools, such as clear acrylic rulers, simplify fabric cutting when paired with a rotary cutter.

4. seam ripper

Even the most experienced sewers make occasional mistakes—that's when a seam ripper comes in handy. This tool has a hooked blade, allowing it to slip easily underneath stitches and cut away unwanted seams.

5. temporary marking pens

Erasable pencils and air- and water-soluble marking pens are used for temporarily marking cutting lines, seam allowances, and other measurements onto fabric. Always test the pen on fabric scraps before using it on finished pieces.

6. fray prevention

Use a dab of fray-prevention product on the cut edge of fabric, fringe, or trim to prevent fraying and unraveling. Look for products that dry clear.

In a pinch with no scissors in sight? Use nail clippers to cut your thread.

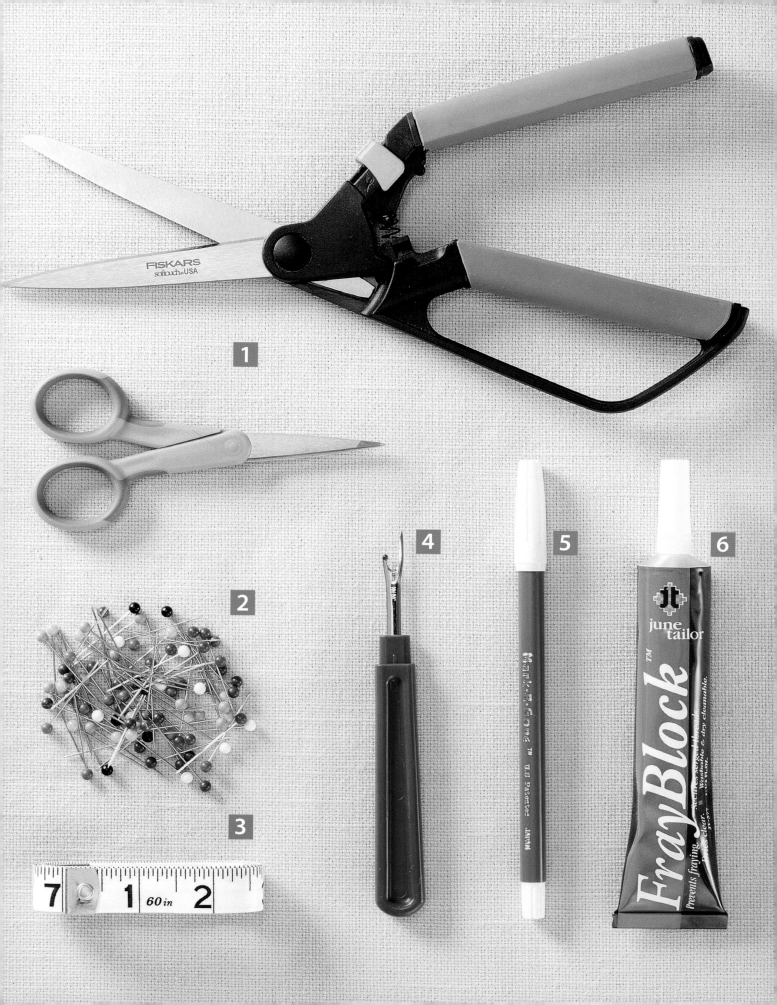

how to buy a sewing machine

How do you know which machine is right for you? Match your skill level, budget, and sewing needs to a machine you'll be happy with for years to come.

These days, purchasing a sewing machine can be almost as involved as buying a car, and sometimes almost as expensive. Technology has transformed the sewing machine, and top-of-the-line computerized models feature hundreds of preprogrammed stitches, dozens of attachments, and in some cases a price tag of $6,000. On the other end of the spectrum, simpler sewing machine models offer just the basics. With such a wide range of choices, how do you know which machine is right for you?

personality profile

If you're in the market for a new machine, perhaps the most important issues to consider are what kind of sewer you are and what types of sewing you do. Beginners may appreciate features such as an automatic bobbin winder or horizontal bobbin, says June Mellinger, director of education for Brother sewing machines.

Jodi Bushman, marketing manager for Janome America, Inc., adds that sewers need to assess their comfort level before choosing a machine. "Some beginners really like to learn how to set tension and stitch length manually," she explains, "while others appreciate a machine that does everything for them. You have to find the machine that suits your personality."

You should also keep fabric preferences in mind. Some inexpensive machines may not handle heavy upholstery or outdoor fabrics.

If you're a quilter or would like to expand your sewing to include more quilting, then look for machines with features that suit that technique. Programmed settings, specialty presser feet, and attachments that expand the sewing area are just a few of the elements found on sewing machines designed for quilters.

Garment sewers may have a separate checklist of preferences. Embroidery and embellishment stitches, automatic tension and stitch lengths, and other details are must-have features for many garment sewers. Sergers are also popular with sewers who are looking for a professional finish to their projects. For more on sergers, see the sidebar opposite.

Once you have your checklist of sewing preferences in hand, the next step, says Nancy Jewell, Publicity Director for Viking USA, is to find a reputable dealer. "Buy the dealer, not the brand. A reputable dealer will provide you with great after-sale customer service, creative inspiration, and helpful instruction through classes, and will be there for you years down the road."

what can you afford?

Now for the tough part—how much can you spend? With machines ranging in price from $99 to $6,000, it's hard to know where to start. The Home Sewing Association (HSA) recommends that you "define your budget and stick to it, and be realistic about your financial commitment." The association points out that limiting your budget too strictly might not get you the accessories that you want or need, but overspending might lead you to feel guilty or

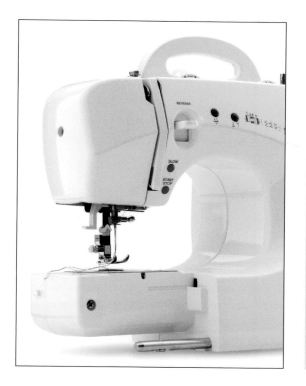

should I buy a serger?

Sewers in the market for a new sewing machine may wonder if buying a serger is worth the extra investment.

Sergers cut and finish the raw edge of the fabric at the same time, giving a professional look to the inside of a project. In recent years, however, manufacturers have added new functions to sergers that show finished edges on the outside.

Although sergers traditionally have been associated with garment sewing, they can create gorgeous home decor and craft projects such as fleece blankets and napkins—fast.

overwhelmed by the investment you've made. Jewell agrees, and adds that you should consider what the price of the machine includes. If a higher-priced machine also includes a thorough warranty, a service plan, and other features that will help you enjoy your machine for many years, then perhaps the extra money is worth it. In addition, ask a dealer if he or she sells used machines. Many used models are in excellent working condition, and some still carry warranties or service plans.

sample the wares

Next, take several machines for a "test drive." The best way to become familiar with a sewing machine is to sew on it. Carry a notebook to the store with you, and after you sample an assortment of stitches (the HSA recommends four to six per machine), make notes about how the machine sewed and how easy it was to adjust the settings. The HSA adds that you should practice several of the same stitches when reviewing different models and brands.

Remember to bring swatches of the fabrics you sew on at home, too. Fabrics provided at the store may be stiff, which shows different stitches well but doesn't indicate how the machine will perform on softer or stretchier fabrics. In addition, use as many of the features on the machine as possible, including threading the machine, changing stitch settings, and winding the bobbin. See if you can execute basic tasks without help from the dealer or salesperson. Finally, review the manual to make sure you can follow the written instructions.

"These are not your mother's machines," says Mellinger. "A lot of things inside the sewing machine have changed. You might have a machine that you found at a garage sale, but the new machines can do so much more. You should find a machine that does what you like it to do now and a little more in the future. That way, as you learn more about sewing, your machine can keep pace with you."

With a little thought about your sewing needs and a bit of research, you can confidently buy a machine that will provide you with years of fun and rewarding sewing.

finding fabrics

Many of the best decorating schemes start with great fabric. Here's what you need to know to find the right fabrics for your home and projects.

Selecting fabrics for your home starts with a clear understanding of the look you're after. Just like people, fabrics express personality. A bright yellow plaid adds a casual, cheery tone to a room, while a gold-threaded brocade connotes elegance.

Keep in mind that the style of your furniture doesn't necessarily dictate the fabrics you choose. In fact, you can give old furniture a whole new look by changing fabrics. For example, a vivid chintz may be just the fabric to loosen up staid Victorian furniture; an elegant damask can change a casual camelback sofa into a luxurious piece.

start looking

To find the ideal fabric, first look at decorating centers, upholstery and drapery shops, and fabrics stores. Check the telephone book for designer fabrics stores as well as for outlets, which may offer overruns or closeouts (be sure to inspect goods carefully; some may be second quality or slightly flawed). Don't forget mail-order catalogs as well as wallpaper books, which may offer coordinating fabrics.

Look for decorative, not garment, fabrics. Decorative fabrics are constructed to be more durable for home furnishings and are usually sold in widths of 48 or 54 inches.

do your research

When you shop, take along samples of carpet, other fabrics, wall coverings, and paints used in your home. As you look through swatch books, remember that small swatches may be misleading: A mini print that looks crisp up close may blur together when you see it on a bed across a room.

Once you've found a fabric you like, take a large sample home. Hang or lay the sample where you intend to use it, and observe how the fabric changes in different light. For drapery material, gently pleat or gather the sample in your hand to see how the pattern is affected.

When you buy or order fabric, purchase all you need at once so you won't have to supplement it later with fabric from a different dye lot. Most design centers and fabrics stores can help you determine how much fabric your project requires.

For items that need to be washed frequently, look for easy-care fabrics, such as cotton or synthetics, that don't need to be dry-cleaned.

Fabric options are more vast and varied than ever. To help winnow your choices to a manageable handful, we've compiled a glossary of the most popular home-decor fabrics. The magic of any fabric lies in its fiber—learn more about the five basic fibers below. Then cozy up to the world of fabrics.

MAN-MADE Nonnatural fibers are appreciated for their drape and easy care. Blended with natural fibers, synthetics boost a fabric's strength, longevity, and wrinkle-resistance. Classics include nylon, rayon, and polyester.

WOOL Baa! We all know wool comes from sheep shearings. Its best feature may be its natural elasticity, which makes it an excellent choice for upholstery. On windows, wool's insulating quality makes it a smart choice. Wool fibers have a spiral shape that, when woven, creates air pockets that serve as insulation against winter chills and summer sun.

LINEN Made from the flax plant, linen is crisp and clean—a popular choice for traditional rooms. Yet in the same way that a linen shirt looks great with blue jeans, linen's uneven fibers and organic grace make it a lovely choice for casual settings. Sunlight can weaken its natural fibers: Extend its life with linings and interlinings. (Linen and cotton are often blended to get the best attributes of each.)

COTTON Plucked from cotton plants in tufts, cotton is a designer's best fabric friend. It is woven into a wide range of patterns, colors, weights, and textures. It also readily accepts applications that make it resistant to flame, water, stains, and shrinking.

SILK Silk's reputation for luxury started long ago in China, where threads spun by silkworms were tapped for fine garments.

choosing a needle

Understanding the terminology associated with machine needles will help take the mystery out of making your selection.

You may think one sewing machine needle is the same as the next. To ensure your stitching success, however, choose the needle best suited for the project at hand. The right needle will make your sewing go more smoothly and may enhance the look of your finished project.

the needle

As shown in the diagram at *left*, the upper part of the needle is the shank and the lower part is the shaft. The shank is rounded on the needle front and flat on the back. Insert the needle into the machine clamp with the front (rounded part) facing you.

The shaft consists of a groove on the front that guides the thread and an indented scarf on the back that enables the bobbin-case hook to get close to the eye of the needle. Its other two elements, the eye and the point, are key factors that vary and affect the needle's performance with different threads and fabrics.

needle sizes

Most needle packages are marked with both European and American numbering systems, such as 70/10 or 80/12, and the needle itself is usually marked with one or both numbers. Sizes range from the finest 60/8 needles to the heaviest 120/19 needles, and available sizes vary within the different types. Finely woven fabrics require a small needle so it will not make holes in the fabric; a larger needle is necessary to stitch heavy or coarse fabrics. A rule of thumb: The larger the number, the stronger the needle.

needle types

Variances in the needle's shank, eye, and point are the distinguishing characteristics of the following needle types. Although a variety of specialty needles are available, we've listed six of the most common types here.

UNIVERSAL Use this needle with an all-purpose sewing thread for most synthetic or natural woven fabrics.

SHARPS Use this needle type for microfiber fabrics, silks, chintzes, lightweight synthetic suedes, and other smooth, thinly woven fabrics. It's also ideal for topstitching and edgestitching.

BALLPOINT Use this needle type for knits made of synthetic or natural fibers. The needle tip is more rounded than the universal needle and goes between the fabric fibers instead of piercing through and breaking them.

LEATHER Use this needle type for real or faux leather and suede, heavy vinyl, and plastic. It has a wedge-shape point that pierces unyielding fabrics without tearing them.

DENIM Use this needle for tightly woven, tough fabrics such as denim, canvas, heavy linen, and duck cloth and for heavy faux leather, vinyl, or waxed cloth.

EMBROIDERY Use this needle for machine embroidery with rayon, acrylic, and metallic decorative threads.

tips for success

When stitching, always check to make sure the needle is inserted correctly and fully. A needle that is not fully inserted into the needle clamp or inserted backwards will not stitch properly or at all. Use your machine's screwdriver to loosen the clamp, then insert the needle fully and use the screwdriver to tighten it in place.

Always use a new needle for each project and replace it after long periods of stitching. A needle that is dull or has a burr may result in broken threads, snagged fabrics, or skipped stitches.

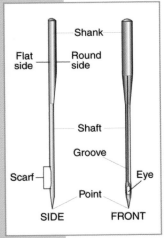

Shank
Flat side
Round side
Shaft
Groove
Scarf
Eye
Point
SIDE
FRONT

ANATOMY OF A MACHINE NEEDLE

unraveling
thread types

There's more to choosing thread than merely matching a color. Because no single thread type can do it all, learn how to choose the right thread for the best results for all your sewing projects.

all-purpose (cotton-covered polyester core) thread

Despite its name, all-purpose thread is not suitable for all sewing projects. It is, however, the most commonly used thread because its polyester core provides strength and stretch while the cotton outer layer allows for smoother, easier sewing. Use it with natural or synthetic, knit or woven fabrics. It's sized for hand stitching, or machine or general purpose sewing.

upholstery, button, and craft thread

For heavy-duty hand and machine sewing, choose an upholstery, button, or craft thread. These threads are the strongest and heaviest of the sewing threads, and their special glazed finish prevents thread abrasion and tangling. They're ideal for tufting buttons on cushions, finishing upholstery, or attaching trim or braid to rugs.

rayon thread

For decorative or machine-embroidery stitching, rayon thread is a good option. Rayon thread has a shiny texture that gives it a silklike appearance. It comes in a variety of solid and variegated colors. Use 40- or 30-weight thread in the needle with a finer-weight thread in the bobbin for machine embroidery and other decorative effects. Read the manufacturer's instructions for special care of rayon threads.

silk thread

This strong, lustrous thread is among the more expensive threads available. It's made from long, continuous filament fibers and has a beautiful sheen. Because it stretches, it's a good choice for tailoring and garment construction. Use 50-weight thread for all-purpose machine sewing, 100-weight thread for appliqué and fine heirloom sewing, and 30-weight thread for topstitching, quilting, or embroidery.

metallic thread

Glittery in appearance, metallic thread is most often used for decorative stitching, but it also makes an attractive choice for satin stitching or machine quilting. It is available in an array of solid and variegated colors and can be used for conventional or overlock machine sewing. With overlock sewing, use the metallic thread in the loopers and a more conventional sewing thread in the needles. Read the manufacturer's instructions for special care of metallic threads.

100% cotton thread

Once the mainstay of home-sewing projects, 100% cotton threads have become less popular because of the improved durability and versatility of other thread types. Best used for hand or machine sewing on such natural-fiber woven fabrics as cotton and linen is 100% cotton mercerized thread. It is smooth, lustrous, and colorfast, and has little stretch. It's ideal for quilting on cotton fabrics.

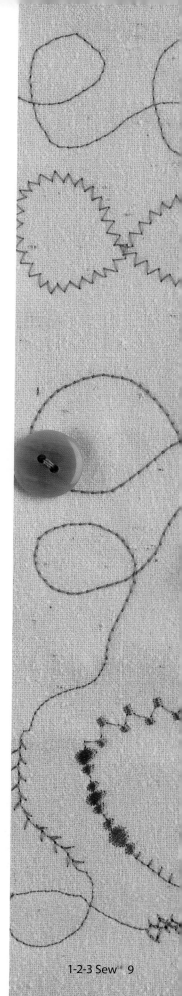

sewing101

Never sewn a stitch? Don't fret—here's all you need to know to sew with confidence. Once you know the basics, you'll soon be on your way to creating custom-made projects with ease.

before you start

FAMILIARIZE YOURSELF WITH YOUR MACHINE

Understanding your machine's features can help you avoid problems or fix them when they arise. Your machine's manual is the best resource for specific information and problem solving. Some basic information applicable to most sewing machines follows.

HOW MACHINES STITCH

The seams created by machine are a series of lockstitches or knots. To create lockstitches on most machines, the thread runs from the spool through tension discs and into the take-up lever. As the needle goes down into the bobbin case, the take-up lever also moves down. In the bobbin case, the bobbin hook creates a loop that interlaces with the thread coming through the needle eye. As the take-up lever and needle come back up through the fabric, the loop formed with the bobbin and needle threads is pulled up to create a stitch. Refer to your machine's manual to learn how to properly thread your needle and wind the bobbin.

PRESSER FEET

These removable accessories (see photo, *below left*) hold the fabric in place against the machine bed and accommodate the needle. Today, even many of the most basic sewing machines come with a variety of presser feet, such as a buttonhole, a blind-hem, and a zipper foot. Check your sewing machine's manual for descriptions and instructions for the presser feet that are available for your machine.

SETTING SEAM GUIDES

The throat plate on your sewing machine—the metal plate below the feed dogs with an opening for the needle to pass through (see photo, *below right*)—is engraved with markings for most common seam guides. Be sure you select the correct throat plate for your sewing needs. For instance, choose a straight-stitch throat plate for straight stitching. For zigzag stitching, use a plate with a wider needle hole to accommodate the side-to-side action of a zigzag stitch.

On many machines, the distance between the needle and the right edge of the presser foot is ¼", a common seam allowance in patchwork and quilting. For seams not indicated on the throat plate, measure the distance from the needle and mark it with a piece of masking tape running parallel to the lines on the throat plate.

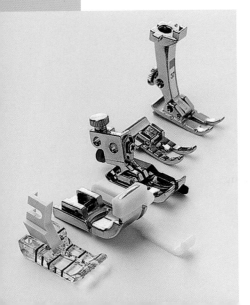

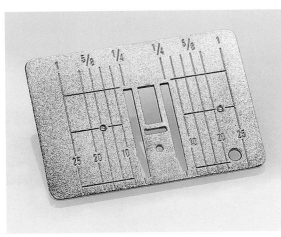

practice sewing

If you've never sewn with a machine before, get a feel for the foot petal and guide the fabric through your machine. Guide the fabric with one hand on the fabric in front of the presser foot and the other hand on the fabric to the left of the presser foot (see photo, *right top*). Don't pull or push the fabric—let the motion of the machine guide the fabric through at a steady pace to the opposite edge. Keep the edge of the fabric in line with the appropriate seam-allowance marking.

prepare the fabric
FIND THE FABRIC GRAIN

Cutting pieces according to a fabric's grain line makes for more accurate piecing and a stronger finished piece. Following the grain line reduces stretching and distortion, enhancing the overall appearance of your completed project. Refer to the diagram *below* to find the grain of your fabric piece.

The arrow on the pattern piece or template indicates which direction the fabric grain should run. Because one or more straight sides of every fabric piece should follow the lengthwise or crosswise grain, it is important that the line on the pattern or template runs parallel to the grain.

The lengthwise grain runs parallel to the tightly woven finished edge, or selvage, and is sometimes referred to as the straight grain. It has the least amount of stretch and is the strongest and smoothest grain.

The crosswise grain runs perpendicular to the selvage. It is usually looser and has slightly more stretch than the lengthwise grain.

True bias intersects the lengthwise grain and crosswise grain at a 45-degree angle, but any line that runs diagonally between the two

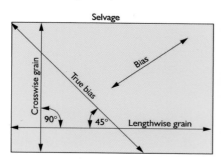

grain lines is called the bias. It has more stretch and flexibility than either the crosswise or lengthwise grain.

When the lengthwise grain and the crosswise grain intersect at a perfect right angle, the fabric is said to be on grain, or grain perfect. Slightly off-grain fabric is still usable.

CUTTING

There are two basic methods for cutting pieces for sewing projects. Cut squares and rectangles using a rotary cutter, an acrylic ruler, and a cutting mat (see photo, *right bottom*). Using the circular cutting tool ensures a quick, accurate way to cut straight lines.

For patterns with curves or odd shapes, pin the pattern to the fabric and use scissors to cut around a pattern. Align the fabric's grain lines so they run parallel to the fabric grain markings on the pattern before cutting out the pieces. Transfer any necessary markings, such as placement markings, from the pattern to the wrong side of the fabric.

PINNING AND BASTING

For accurate seaming, pin fabric pieces together before sewing. Unless otherwise indicated, place pieces with right sides together, aligning the raw edges, and pin the pieces together along the edges. Insert the pins perpendicular to the edges. When sewing a seam, avoid sewing over the pins by removing them as you sew.

Pinning pieces together is often a sufficient way to temporarily join pieces before sewing. However, if you have a more complicated seam to sew, such as a zipper, thread basting is a helpful way to secure the pieces together. You can baste your pieces together by threading a sewing needle with a double length of contrasting sewing thread and using long running stitches where the permanent stitch line will be. After the pieces are machine-sewn, remove the basting stitches.

start sewing

SEAM ALLOWANCES

Before sewing, note the seam allowances for your particular project. They usually range from ¼" to ⅝".

STARTING AND ENDING SEAMS

To secure the thread ends when beginning and ending a seam, it's necessary to backstitch. To start a seam, position the needle ⅝" in from the edge. Use the reverse function on your machine to backstitch to the edge, then stitch forward along the seam line. Repeat when finishing the seam line (see diagram, *below*).

When finishing intersecting seams, such as a circle, overlap the stitching over the beginning of the stitch the same distance as the backstitch at the beginning of the seam.

PIVOTING AROUND CORNERS

To continue a seam around a corner, stop in the needle-down position ⅝" from the edge (you may need to adjust the position of the needle by turning the wheel on your machine toward you). Lift the presser foot and turn the fabric until the new fabric edge is aligned with the appropriate seam guideline on the throat plate. Lower the presser foot and continue sewing along the new edge.

SNIPPING SEAMS

After you've finished sewing the basic seams, snip the raw edges of the seam allowance to reduce the bulk and prevent puckering. Here are options for snipping three basic seam types:

for straight seams: Press open the seam, and snip notches at intervals in the selvage, *below left.*

for corners: Cut diagonally across the corner, then make additional angled cuts close to the stitching line, *below right.* Don't cut too close, however, or the stitches might pull out when your pillow is stuffed (especially during those vigorous pillow fights).

for concave curves: Snip notches along the curve to reduce the bulk and tension, *bottom.* Use this technique when making bolsters or round pillows.

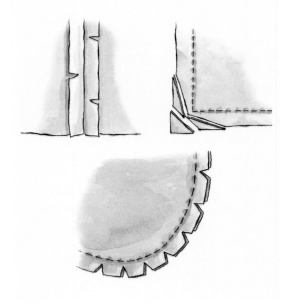

finishing details

Practice these secrets from experienced sewers to give your projects polish and panache.

straightening the grain

Sometimes the fabric you buy will have a pattern that does not run straight with the grain of the fabric. Determining the straight grain before you measure or cut will help you avoid future problems.

Working from one cut edge of the fabric, gently pull on a crosswise grain thread, with the intent of pulling that thread out from the fabric's weave. The pulled thread will reveal the true grain of the fabric.

It may be necessary to unravel several threads before being able to pull one thread that spans the entire width of fabric. The thread may break in the process of pulling. Depending on how far through the crosswise grain the thread has been pulled, the correct crosswise straight of grain may have become visible, even though the thread has broken. If not, start again with another thread.

Using scissors, cut the fabric on the "exposed" correct crosswise grain. Use this "line" to make straight cuts on the fabric for pillows, curtains, or other home accessories.

finishing

Clean-finishing the seam allowance edges will help prevent unraveling and provide a professional finish.

A great all-purpose finishing method is to zigzag-stitch each edge of the seam. Use a medium-length stitch.

For light-wear items or fray-resistant fabrics such as wool, use pinking shears to trim away ¼" of the seam allowances on both layers at the same time; press the seam open.

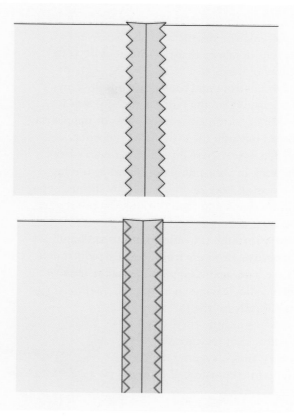

If the thread breaks or your sewing machine is stitching poorly, skipping, or making uneven stitches, try rethreading the machine, replacing the needle, or using a new spool of thread.

covering buttons

A covered button is a perfect focal point in a pillow center. Start with a kit for covering buttons, available in the notions department at a fabrics store. Numerous sizes are available; larger sizes (1 to 2 inches) are easiest to work with and lend drama to your project.

From fabric scraps, cut a circle ⅝ inch larger than the button form. Baste around the circle, using large stitches and leaving long thread tails, *above*. Fold the fabric over the base, gathering threads tightly and securing with a knot. Position the button back over the covered top, *below*, pressing firmly.

tufting with covered buttons

Following the instructions above, cover two buttons in fabrics that coordinate with your pillow or cushion.

On the front and back of your pillow, mark the spots where the buttons will go. Slip a length of cotton embroidery floss or upholstery thread through the eye of a long needle; double it over. Sew on matching marks from the back of your pillow to the front, leaving the threads long on the back. Sew through one button shank and then through the pillow to the back again.

Sew through the other button shank and then through to the front, *below*. Sew through to the back again. Clip the thread to remove the needle, leaving ends long. Pull tightly on the threads so the buttons sink into the fabrics. Tightly knot the threads several times, keeping them taut while knotting. Trim the excess threads.

finishing french seams

Use this seam technique when working with sheer fabrics where sewing lines and raw edges show through. Sew the fabrics with the wrong sides together, using a ¼-inch seam allowance. Trim the seam ⅛ inch from the sewing line, *below top*. To enclose the raw edge, turn the fabric wrong side out, press, and sew ⅜ inch from the edge, *below bottom*.

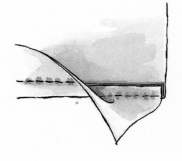

Press, don't iron. Pressing a project means putting the iron on the fabric, then picking it up to move it. Ironing, or sliding the iron back and forth, causes stretching.

---

eliminating misshapen corners

To make professional-looking, tailored corners on pillows that have corners sewn at right angles, slightly taper the raw edges at the corners, *below*. Trim away ½ inch of each corner with a gradual angle that begins 3½ inches from the corner at each perpendicular side. Sew the corner seam using the tapered edges.

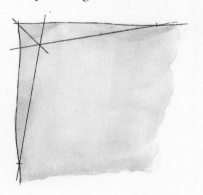

filling pillows

When your pillow is sewn and ready to be stuffed, you can plump it up in several ways. **pillow forms** are one of the easiest ways to fill your pillows. You can purchase them in myriad shapes and sizes—even cubes and balls. For the softest, cushiest pillows, choose down-filled forms. They cost a bit more, but you'll love the results. Tailor the size of your form to the fullness you desire for your pillow; for the fullest shape, choose a pillow form that's the same size or even slightly larger than the size of your pillow cover.

fiberfill is another option. This filler can get a little lumpy, so smooth it into the final shape before stuffing it into your pillow.

for square or box shapes, you also can use thick foam. Cut the foam with a serrated knife and insert it into your pillow.

To eliminate fraying when you sew with loosely woven fabrics, such as a linen, overcast the edge of the seam allowance after the seam is sewn. Use a zigzag stitch on your sewing machine to enclose the raw edges.

gathering ruffles

To make homespun ruffles, start with a strip of fabric twice the length of the finished ruffle (for example, twice the circumference or perimeter of a pillow). The strip should be as wide as you want your finished ruffle to be, plus 1 inch for the hem and seam allowance.

Press under one long edge ¼ inch. Press under ¼ inch again; top-stitch the hem in place. Machine-baste ⅜ inch from the other (unfinished) long edge. Machine-baste another line ¼ inch from the first basting line (*Diagram 1*). The second line should be closer to the unfinished edge than the first.

Pull threads of both basting lines to create gathers, pulling gently and evenly along the length of the fabric (*Diagram 2*).

With right sides together and the raw edges aligned, pin the ruffle to the fabric (*Diagram 3*), evening out gathers; sew using a ½-inch seam allowance. Remove the basting. Finish the project as directed.

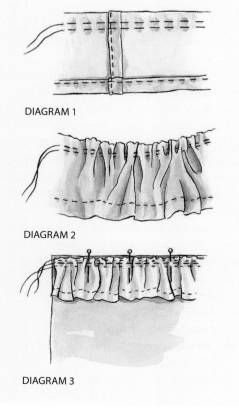

DIAGRAM 1

DIAGRAM 2

DIAGRAM 3

bind it right

Double-layer binding is easy to apply and adds durability to a finished quilt or sewn project.

cut the strips

Unless otherwise specified in the project, cut the binding on the straight grain of the fabric (for details, see page 17). The cutting instructions for each project tell you the width and how many binding strips to cut. Join the binding strips with diagonal seams (see photo, *left top*) to make one long binding strip. Trim the seam allowances to ¼ inch; press the seams open.

attach the binding

With the wrong side inside, fold under 1 inch at one end of the binding strip and press. Then fold the strip in half lengthwise with the wrong side inside. Place the binding strip against the right side of the quilt top along one edge, aligning the binding strip's raw edges with the quilt top's raw edge (do not start at a corner). Begin sewing the binding in place 2 inches from the folded end (see photo, *left bottom*).

turn the corner

Stop sewing when you're ¼ inch from the corner (or a distance equal to the seam allowance you're using). Backstitch, then clip the threads (see *photo 1, right top*). Remove the project from under the presser foot.

Fold the binding strip upward, creating a diagonal fold, and finger-press (see *photo 2, right center*).

Holding the diagonal fold in place with your finger, bring the binding strip down in line with the next edge, making a horizontal fold that aligns with the quilt edge. Start sewing again at the top of the horizontal fold, stitching through all layers (see *photo 3, right bottom*). Sew around the quilt, turning each corner in the same manner.

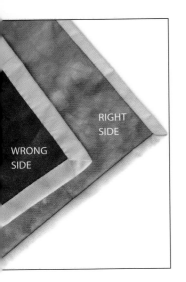

WRONG SIDE

RIGHT SIDE

1

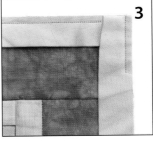

2

3

finish it up

When you return to the starting point, encase the binding strip's raw edge inside the folded end and finish sewing to the starting point. Trim the batting and backing fabric even with the quilt top edges.

Turn the binding over the edge to the back. Hand-stitch the binding to the backing fabric only, covering any machine stitching. To make binding corners on the quilt back, match the mitered corners on the quilt front, hand-stitch up to a corner, and make a fold in the binding. Secure the fold with two stitches; then continue stitching the binding in place along the next edge.

piping basics

Similar to piped icing on a cake, corded piping makes an attractive finishing touch for many home-decorating projects. You can easily customize it to match virtually any project when you carefully select coordinating fabric to encase the piping cord.

Corded piping consists of a bias strip sewn around cotton cording. A flange formed by the seam allowance lets the piping be sewn into the seam of a project, lending it a professional finish.

1. find the bias

Cutting strips on the bias makes the fabric easier to wrap around the cording and around corners of your finished project. To find the bias (a line diagonal to the grain of the fabric), make sure the edges of your fabric are cut along the grain. Fold one of the corners diagonally across the fabric, and finger-press the fold. The pressed line is the bias line.

2. cut the strips

Align a clear acrylic ruler along the pressed line at the width you want to cut your bias strips. The cut width of the bias strips should equal the diameter of the cord plus 1 inch for seam allowances. Use a rotary cutter to cut the strips along the edge of the ruler.

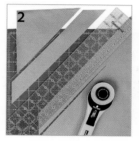

3. join the strips

With right sides together, lay the strips at right angles to each other. Pin and sew diagonally 3/16 inch from the edge. Open and press the seam flat. Trim away the corners that extend beyond the strip edge.

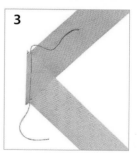

4. wrap the cord

Lay the cord in the center of the wrong side of the bias strip. Fold and pin the fabric over the cord, aligning the raw edges. Using a zipper or piping foot attachment on your sewing machine, sew close to the cord along the length of the strip. The stitching should tightly encase the cord. Do not trim the seam allowance—it will be used to attach the piping to the project. Cut the required length of piping for your project, adding 4 inches for each joined length if needed.

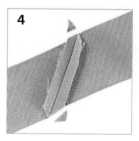

5. attach the piping

Lay the piping on the right side of the fabric, aligning the raw cut-edge of the piping with the raw cut-edge of the fabric. Position the piping so the rounded side faces the center of the project; pin in place. Using a zipper- or piping-foot attachment on your sewing machine, baste the piping in place. To overlap two piping ends, unravel each end of the cording and cut out approximately half of the strands. Twist the two ends together, and hand-stitch around the twisted joint to hold it together. Re-cover the cording, folding the raw edge of the top strip under.

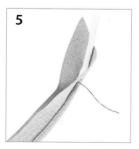

With right sides facing, lay the backing panel on top of the panel with the attached piping. Using the basted seam line as a guide, sew through all fabric layers. If the project requires turning, leave an opening along one of the sides. Turn the project to the right side and stuff if required. Using a slip stitch, hand-sew the opening closed.

trim into shape

Get the skinny on decorative trims—what they're called and how to use them.

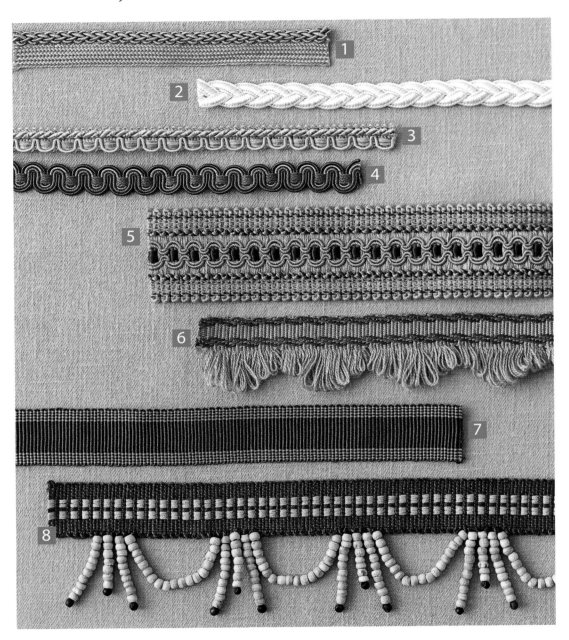

gimps, braids, & tapes

GIMP (1, 2, 3, and 4) is a flat, narrow trim (usually less than a half inch wide) and commonly used to cover upholstery tacks or to embellish draperies, pillows, and cushions. Some gimp is shaped in a SCALLOP (4) pattern. A GALLOON (5) is an elaborately woven, very wide type of gimp that often contains metallic threads. It is used to edge draperies, valances, cornices, and skirts of upholstered furniture. BRAID (6) is a wider and flatter version of a gimp and often has embroidered details. TAPE (7 and 8) has a flat, smooth weave and is used to create borders on pillows, slipcovers, draperies, and upholstery. Some are embellished with a fringe of threads or beads.

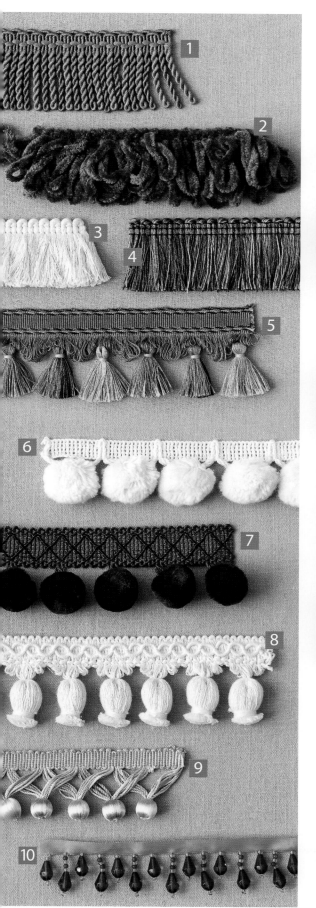

fringes

Fringe consists of a heading (where the strands are sewn together at the top) and a skirt (the strands that hang from the heading). The threads can be cut, looped, or twisted, or they may support beads or tassels. Headings may be plain and meant to be sewn into a seam, or elaborate and sewn on top of the fabric. Fringe is used to edge draperies, window shades, table skirts, pillows, and lampshades. Common types of fringes (see photo, *left*) include **BULLION (1), LOOP (2), BRUSH (3 and 4), TASSEL (5), POM-POM (6 and 7), ONION TASSEL (8), BALL (9), AND BEADED (10).**

piping & cords

Piping and cord are usually used to reinforce and define seams for a clean, tailored look. **PIPING (1)**, also called welting, is made of cord encased in strips of bias-cut fabric or ribbon (see photo, above). **CORD (2–9)**, also called cable, is usually made of two or more strands twisted or plaited together. It often has a flange, the flat band of fabric that allows it to be sewn into a seam. Cord takes on many different looks, depending on the materials used, the number of strands, and how they are twisted together. Look for cords ranging from simple and **MONOCHROMATIC (2 AND 3)** to **MULTICOLOR (4)** to **COMPLEX DESIGNS** in which each strand itself has a different pattern **(5 AND 6)**. Unexpected materials, such as **METALLIC THREADS (7), SUEDE (8), AND LEATHER (9)**, woven into geometric patterns are a contemporary take on traditional cording.

a lesson worth repeating

You've found the perfect floral print—now how do you match the patterns for a seamless look to your project? Before you buy your fabric, learn the ins and outs of working with pattern repeats.

A pattern repeat is the distance from the starting point of a design on the fabric to the place where that design starts over again, repeating itself. For example, if the repeat is 12 inches and includes a flower along the edge, the top of that flower will be at the same position every 12 inches along the edge.

the basics

The pattern repeat is listed on the fabric sample tag when fabric is ordered from a sample book or a fabric retailer. When purchasing the fabric off a bolt, simply measure from one specific point in the pattern to where it occurs again. A common pattern repeat is 27 inches, but pattern repeats can be as little as 2 or 3 inches and larger than 36 inches.

When making a window treatment or other project that uses wide widths of fabric, such as the ones *opposite,* it's critical to allow enough fabric for the pattern repeat so the design will continue uninterrupted when pieces of fabric are sewn side by side. For example, if half of a vase is on one selvage of the fabric, the other half of the vase will be on the other selvage. When the two pieces are sewn together, the vase is complete. Most printed fabrics are designed this way.

For professional-looking results, always match patterns. This goes for multiple window treatments in a room, as well as within the same window treatment. From window to window in a room the motifs should match, or

fall at the same height, on every treatment.

To allow for pattern repeat on a window treatment, you have to know how much fabric to buy. First, determine the length of fabric you will need for each piece, including the header and the hem. Then, use the pattern repeat formula explained in Figuring Pattern Repeats, opposite, and Figuring a Drop Pattern on page 22, to determine how much extra fabric is needed to match the design in every cut. The same rules apply for other projects that require sewing fabrics side by side.

picking the perfect print

Understanding what pattern repeat is and why it's important is only half the key to pattern success. You also need to choose the right print—with the right pattern repeat—for your project.

To do so, determine the finished width and length of the project, as well as the size of each section. For instance, if a shade is 36 inches wide, it may have three 12-inch-wide sections. If a shade will almost always be drawn, determine its length in that position. Next, determine the placement of the design on the treatment (commonly centered horizontally and vertically in each section).

Based on these decisions and measurements, evaluate the pattern scale and repeat on the fabrics you are considering. A motif that is wider or longer than each section of the window treatment will not be seen completely, losing the desired effect and perhaps making the fabric look entirely different. On the other hand, be aware that a small pattern can get lost in large or full treatment sections. Viewing a small pattern on a window at a distance can make it disappear, or cause colors to blend.

Take note of how a pattern repeats across the width of the fabric. If it does not repeat to coordinate with your measurements or does not repeat at all, the same design cannot be centered in each section. Also, consider the fullness of the treatment: The more fullness, the less the pattern will show. If you want to feature a specific motif, consider a window treatment that is flat or has flat sections to highlight the design.

figuring pattern repeats

If the fabric is cut to the exact length needed to make the window treatment, there will be enough fabric. But when the second piece of fabric is brought up to be sewn beside the first, the designs may not match. Each piece must be cut at the repeat of the design, so the design at the top of the fabric is the same on all pieces.

To determine at what measurement to cut all the pieces of fabric so the pattern is identical, follow this simple three-step formula and refer to the illustration on *page 22*. Our example is based on a needed length of 96 inches.

1. Divide the desired length of each piece of fabric (96 inches) by the size of the repeat. For a pattern repeat of 27 inches, 96 inches divided by 27 inches equals 3.6. This means there are 3.6 repeats of the 27-inch pattern within the 96-inch length.

2. Round up to the next whole number (4), because you need whole repeats.

3. Multiply the size of the repeat (27 inches) by the number of repeats (4). This determines at what length the fabric should be cut to have the same pattern at the top of each piece—at 108 inches, not 96 inches. In this example, the 12 inches beyond the 96-inch length is waste.

When buying, keep in mind that the fabric on the bolt may have been cut at a different location within a repeat than where you would like the pattern in your treatment to begin. To allow for this, add one additional pattern repeat to the overall yardage calculation in order to have enough extra fabric to shift the pattern accordingly. Although this wastes a small amount of fabric, it is worth the effort and expense to have the perfect treatment with the perfect match.

figuring a drop pattern

In a typical pattern repeat, where a design is on one selvage, the rest of the same design is directly across from it on the opposite selvage. Occasionally, you will find a fabric with a drop pattern match (also called a half match or half-drop match) where the remainder of the design is, instead, moved up or down along the opposite selvage at an amount equal to one-half of the pattern repeat (see the illustration *near left*).

To calculate the allowance for matching a drop pattern, follow the steps in Figuring Pattern Repeats on page 21. Then, add or subtract one-half of a repeat. Using the same 96-inch-long example, add or subtract 13½ inches (half of the 27-inch repeat) to/from 108 inches to determine a new cut length of 121½ inches or 94½ inches. Since 96 inches was originally needed to make the treatment, subtracting one-half of a repeat would make the cut too short. In this case, add one-half of the repeat to allow 121½ inches for each cut (in this example, 25½ inches beyond the 96-inch length is waste). If the original amount of fabric needed had been less than 94½ inches, you would have subtracted one-half of a repeat.

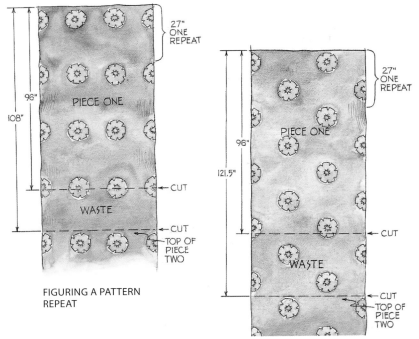

FIGURING A PATTERN REPEAT

FIGURING A DROP PATTERN

terms to know

Refer to these definitions when you are reading project instructions. These key terms cover many of the sewing basics.

BASTING Long stitches made by hand or machine. They are used to hold fabrics together temporarily.

BIAS CUT Fabric that is cut on the diagonal, at 45 degrees to the straight grain.

EASING Process of working in extra fabric where two pieces do not align precisely.

EDGESTITCH A straight stitch made with a machine close to a finished edge, seam, or fold.

FLANGE A border of flat fabric that extends beyond the stitching line around the outer edge of a pillow, sham, or duvet cover.

FUSIBLE WEB Paper-backed adhesive used to fuse fabrics together using a hot iron.

GATHERING STITCH A long running stitch that can be pulled to draw up the fabric into gathers. Usually sewn in pairs close together.

GRAIN Direction the fibers of a fabric are woven. Straight or lengthwise grain runs parallel to the selvages. Crosswise grain runs perpendicular to the straight grain.

HEM Finished lower edge of a project, stitched by hand or with a machine.

HEMSTITCH A stitch done by hand to invisibly tack up a hem. Uses small vertical or slanted stitches that catch a small amount of fabric on the front and a larger amount on the hem.

INTERFACING Placed on the back of a fabric or between fabrics to give shape or stiffness. Choose a weight that matches the fabric being used. Comes in fusible (iron-on) and nonfusible (sew-in) versions.

NOTCH A small V-shape clipped into a curved seam to reduce bulk and make seams lie flat.

NOTIONS Small items used to complete a sewing project, such as zippers, buttons, or trims.

PIPING Trim made from bias-cut strips, often covering a cord. Instructions for making piping are on page 17.

PLEAT A fold of fabric used to gather fabric fullness in a uniform way. Examples: box pleat, knife pleat, inverted pleat, goblet pleat.

RAW EDGE The cut fabric edge that is often finished to prevent raveling.

RIGHT SIDE The side of a fabric that is intended to show on the finished item.

SEAM ALLOWANCE Narrow section of fabric between a stitching line and the edge of the fabric. For home-decor projects, a ½- or ⅝-inch seam allowance is common.

SELVAGE The side edges of the fabric. They are often bound more tightly than the rest of the fabric and may include printing that indicates the manufacturer or product line. Generally, they should be cut off or they may cause seams to pucker.

SLIP STITCH A hand-worked stitch used to attach a folded fabric layer to another layer. Often used to close the opening on a pillow after the form is inserted.

STRAIGHT STITCH Basic machine stitch used for seaming, stay stitching, or topstitching.

TOPSTITCH Straight stitch sewn very close to a finished edge for a decorative effect. Sometimes sewn as a double row or with contrasting thread.

WRONG SIDE Reverse side of a fabric that is usually on the inside of a finished project.

ZIGZAG STITCH A side-to-side machine stitch used to prevent a raw edge from raveling. Can be stitched in varying widths.

piles of pillows

In next to no time, you can have a bed or sofa full of fun pillows in interesting shapes and sizes. Here are instructions for four popular styles. Once you are comfortable with them, experiment with more complicated versions by adding trims and embroidery.

Photographed by Peter Krumhardt

basic square pillows

Ivory pillow shown *opposite* and on *page 27*; green floor pillow shown *opposite.*

MATERIALS
- Pillow form
- Decorator fabric (amount depends on size of the pillow)
- Matching sewing thread
- Piping or beaded trim as desired

All measurements include a ½" seam allowance. Sew with right sides together unless otherwise stated.

INSTRUCTIONS
Determine the size of the pillow form. Measure the pillow, adding ½" on all sides for seam allowances. Cut two pieces of fabric to these measurements. Cut piping or beaded trim to length of perimeter. *(For instructions on how to make matching piping from the fabric, see "Piping Basics" on page 17.)*

On the right side of the pillow top piece, pin piping or trim around the perimeter, matching raw edges, *above right.*

Using a zipper foot and a long stitch length, baste the trim to the pillow top piece (see page 17 for instructions on how to abut the trim ends). Clip the trim seam allowance to help ease it around the corners.

With right sides together, pin pillow bottom piece over pillow top piece, sandwiching trim between layers.

Using a zipper foot and a normal stitch length, stitch the top to the bottom, leaving an opening to insert the pillow form. Turn pillow cover right sides out. Insert form. Slip-stitch opening closed.

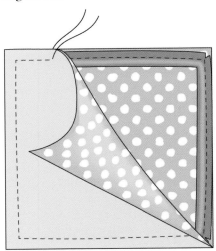

For a luxe look without the effort of hand embroidery, look for fabrics already embellished with stitching and beads.

pillow with gussets

Round pink pillow shown *opposite* and on *page 25*.

MATERIALS

- Pillow form
- Decorator fabric (amount depends on size of the pillow)
- Tailor's chalk or pencil
- Piping or beaded trim as desired
- Matching sewing thread
- Covered buttons (optional)

INSTRUCTIONS

Determine the size of the pillow form and add a ½" seam allowance all around. Use these measurements to cut out two round or square pieces of fabric for the pillow front and back. To make it easier to cut a perfectly round or square shape, trace, measure, and mark the shape on a cardboard template first. Then lay the template on the fabric and mark around the edge with tailor's chalk or a pencil; cut it out.

To figure the length of the gusset or strip, measure the distance around the pillow and add ½" for each seam allowance. For a large pillow, you may have to piece together a couple of strips to get the length you want.

The round pink pillow *opposite* uses beaded trim around the edges to emphasize its shape. Using piping around the perimeter is another attractive way to give your pillow a professional finish. For either of these details, determine the length of piping or trim you will need by multiplying the length of the gusset by 2; add 1". *(For instructions on how to make matching piping, see page 17.)*

Place the gusset right side up. Cut the length of piping or beaded trim in half and pin it to the front of the strip, matching the raw edges. Refer to the placement in *Diagram A*. Stitch in place, making sure not to catch any beaded trim in the seam.

Pin the short ends of the gusset together, right sides facing. Stitch the seam with a ½" seam allowance to make a circle *(Diagram B)*. Trim the seam to about ⅜" and press open.

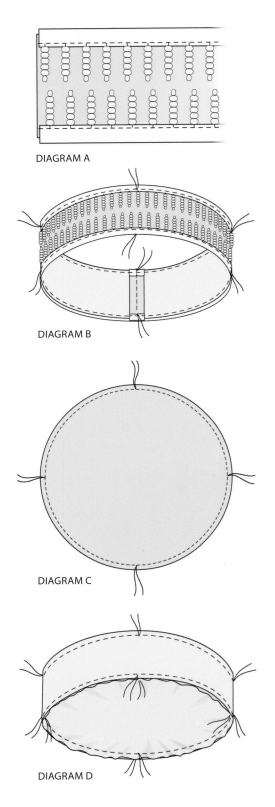

DIAGRAM A

DIAGRAM B

DIAGRAM C

DIAGRAM D

To add an embellishment to your pillow top, attach it before you stitch the fabric sections together. For beaded details, draw a design on unsewn fabric with fabric glue. Use a needle and thread to string beads, and press them onto the glue.

Fold the gusset into quarters and mark each quarter with contrasting thread by making a couple of stitches and leaving long tails.

Fold the top and bottom pillow pieces into quarters and mark each quarter the same way *(Diagram C)*.

Baste ⅜" from the raw edge of the top and bottom pillow pieces. Start and stop the stitching at each quarter mark *(Diagram C)*. With right sides facing, pin the gusset to the top of the pillow, matching quarter marks. Gently pull the threads to ease each of the quarters to fit the gusset *(Diagram D)*. Evenly distribute the gathers and pin the gusset to the pillow. Stitch the top to the gusset using a ½" seam allowance.

Repeat to sew the bottom, leaving a 10" opening. Turn the pillow cover right sides out, press, and insert the pillow form. Hand-sew the opening closed. Add a covered button if desired *(see page 14 for instructions on making covered buttons)*.

tied bolster

Purple neck-roll pillow shown on *page 25*.

MATERIALS
- Bolster form
- Decorator fabric (amount depends on size of the pillow)
- Contrasting fabric for trim
- Matching sewing thread

INSTRUCTIONS

Measure the length and circumference of the bolster form *(Diagram A on page 28)*, adding ½" on all sides for seam allowances. Cut a rectangular piece of fabric to these measurements.

For the tied bolster ends, cut two 8"-wide pieces of fabric that measure the circumference of the bolster plus 1".

For trim, cut two 2"-wide strips of contrasting fabric that measure the circumference of the bolster plus 1".

Fold each trim piece in half lengthwise

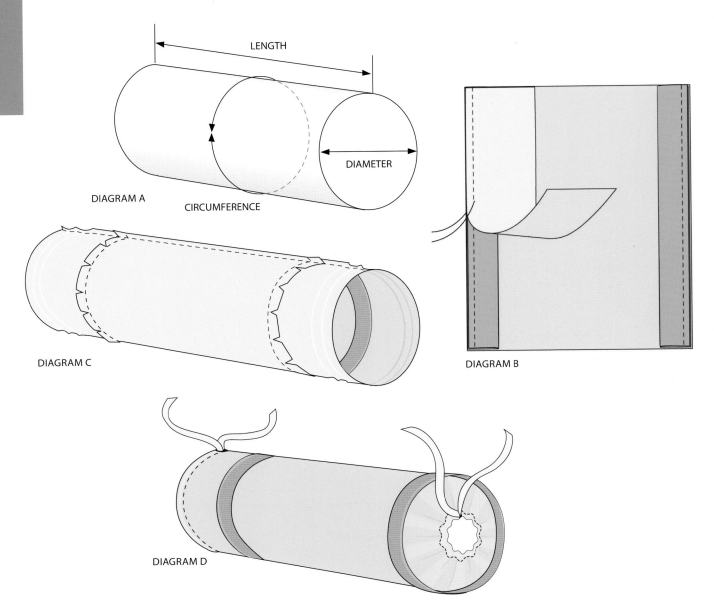

DIAGRAM A

LENGTH

DIAMETER

CIRCUMFERENCE

DIAGRAM C

DIAGRAM B

DIAGRAM D

with wrong sides together; press. With right side of bolster fabric facing up, pin one trim piece to each end of the bolster, aligning raw edges; sew and press.

Sew one long edge of the bolster end to the bolster, right sides together, aligning raw edges and sandwiching trim between the layers *(Diagram B)*. Repeat with the other bolster end piece. Press under ¾" along one long edge of each bolster end. Press under ¾" more; unfold. Snip small notches along the seam allowance, taking care not to cut through the stitching lines.

With right sides together, fold the assembled piece in half, aligning pressed casing lines.

Sew, leaving open the ¾" between casing lines at each end. Turn right side out. Refold casing lines, and stitch ½" from folded edge *(Diagram C)*.

For ties, cut two 2"-wide strips 24" long. Fold each strip in half lengthwise with wrong sides together; press. Unfold and fold in each raw edge to the center pressed line; press.

Refold along center line; press. Edgestitch to enclose the raw edges, turning the short ends in. Tie knot in each end. Repeat for remaining tie.

Thread one tie through the casing at each end of the bolster. Insert bolster form. Pull tie to enclose *(Diagram D)*.

flanged pillow

Striped pillow with pink flanges shown on *page 25*.

MATERIALS

- Pillow form
- Decorator fabric (amount depends on size of the pillow)
- Contrasting fabric for flange
- Matching sewing thread

INSTRUCTIONS

Measure the pillow form, adding ½" on all sides for seam allowances. Cut two pieces of fabric to these measurements. For a 2"-wide flange, cut four 3"-wide strips the height of your pillow. Cut four more 3"-wide strips the width of your pillow plus 5".

With right sides together, sew a strip to each short side of the pillow front. Press seam allowances toward the pillow body. With right sides together, sew a strip to each long side of the pillow front, extending over the flange strips *(Diagram A)*. Press the seam allowances toward the pillow body. Repeat for the pillow back.

With right sides together, sew the pillow front to the pillow back along flange edges, leaving an opening for turning *(Diagram B)*. Turn the pillow right side out.

Pin the pillow front and back together along the line where the flange connects to the pillow body. Sew "in the ditch" along the seam line all the way around the pillow, leaving an opening for inserting the pillow form; press.

Insert the pillow form and machine-stitch the rest of the way around the flange/body seam *(Diagram C)*. If your form fits tightly into the pillow, you may find it easiest to stitch this last section closed using your sewing machine's zipper foot.

Slip-stitch the flange opening closed.

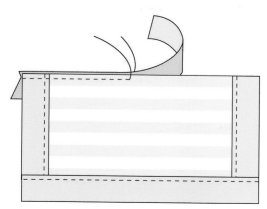

DIAGRAM A

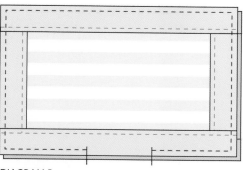

DIAGRAM B

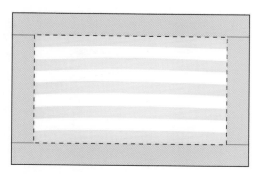

DIAGRAM C

Choose multiple fabrics for a grouping of pillows the no-fail way— look for prints from the same fabric collection. These prematched collections make it a cinch to coordinate the look.

grab**bags**

A simple bag pattern and two fabrics with character equal one fun tote. You'll want to make them by the dozen.

Designed by Bonnie Kozowski   Photographed by Cameron Sadeghpour

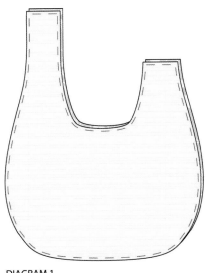

DIAGRAM 1

DIAGRAM 2

Designer Bonnie Kozowski has made countless versions of this go-everywhere bag in a variety of fun prints and colors. Pockets on the inside are great for holding your phone, keys, and other necessities.

Although most of the bags shown are made from quilting cottons, the bag also looks great in denim, tapestry, and upholstery-weight fabrics. (If you use a heavyweight fabric, you don't need to use batting.)

MATERIALS

- ½ yard print A (bag)
- ¾ yard print B (lining)
- 18×44" thin quilt batting or craft fleece

finished bag:
13×18"
quantities are for 44/45"-wide, 100% cotton fabrics. All measurements include a ¼" seam allowance. Sew with right sides together unless otherwise stated.

CUT FABRICS

To make the best use of your fabrics, cut pieces in the following order. The Bag Pattern is on *page 34*. To make a template of the pattern, enlarge it by 185%, trace it onto a large sheet of paper, and cut out. Be sure to transfer the clips and dots onto the template, then to the fabric pieces.

From print A, cut:
- 1 *each* of Bag Pattern and Bag Pattern reversed

From print B, cut:
- 1 *each* of Bag Pattern and Bag Pattern reversed
- 2—6½×15" rectangles

From batting, cut:
- 2 of Bag Pattern

PREPARE BAG PIECES AND POCKETS

1. Layer a batting bag piece on wrong side of each A print bag piece. Machine-baste a scant ¼" from edges to make bag front and back *(Diagram 1, above)*.

2. Fold a B print 6½×15" rectangle in half lengthwise to make a 3¼×15" rectangle. Sew together along three open edges, leaving a 3" opening for turning in the bottom edge *(Diagram 2, above)*. Turn right side out through opening. Press, turning under raw edges of

opening, to make a pocket. Repeat to make a second pocket.

3. Position a pocket on the right side of each B print bag piece at the widest part; pin in place. Referring to *Diagram 3, opposite*, topstitch bottom edge of each pocket, then stitch two vertical lines 5" apart to divide each pocket into compartments. Trim pocket side edges along curve of bag piece; baste a scant ¼" from edges to make lining front and back.

ASSEMBLE BAG

1. With right sides together, sew together bag front and back from clip to clip along side and bottom edges *(Diagram 4, opposite)*. Clip into seam allowance where marked. Turn bag right side out; press flat.

2. Repeat Step 1 to sew together lining front and back, leaving an opening for turning between the dots in the bottom seam *(Diagram 5, opposite)*. Do not turn right side out.

DIAGRAM 3

DIAGRAM 4

DIAGRAM 5

DIAGRAM 6

DIAGRAM 7

DIAGRAM 8

3. Insert bag body into lining (they will be right sides together). Sew together bag body and lining along inside and outside edges, beginning and ending 2" from top edges *(Diagram 6, above)*. Pull bag and lining through opening in lining bottom. Hand–stitch opening closed. Push bag into lining so the bag is wrong side out.

4. On the lining, carefully press under ¼" on the handle upper edges. Keeping the lining out

of the way, pin together the long handle ends of the bag body; stitch with ½" seam allowance *(Diagram 7, above)*. Repeat to join the bag body short handle ends.

5. Turn in remaining raw edges of handles on the bag body and lining (the lining handle ends should overlap each other); pin in place. Turn right side out. Topstitch around all edges to secure the handle ends and complete the bag *(Diagram 8, above)*.

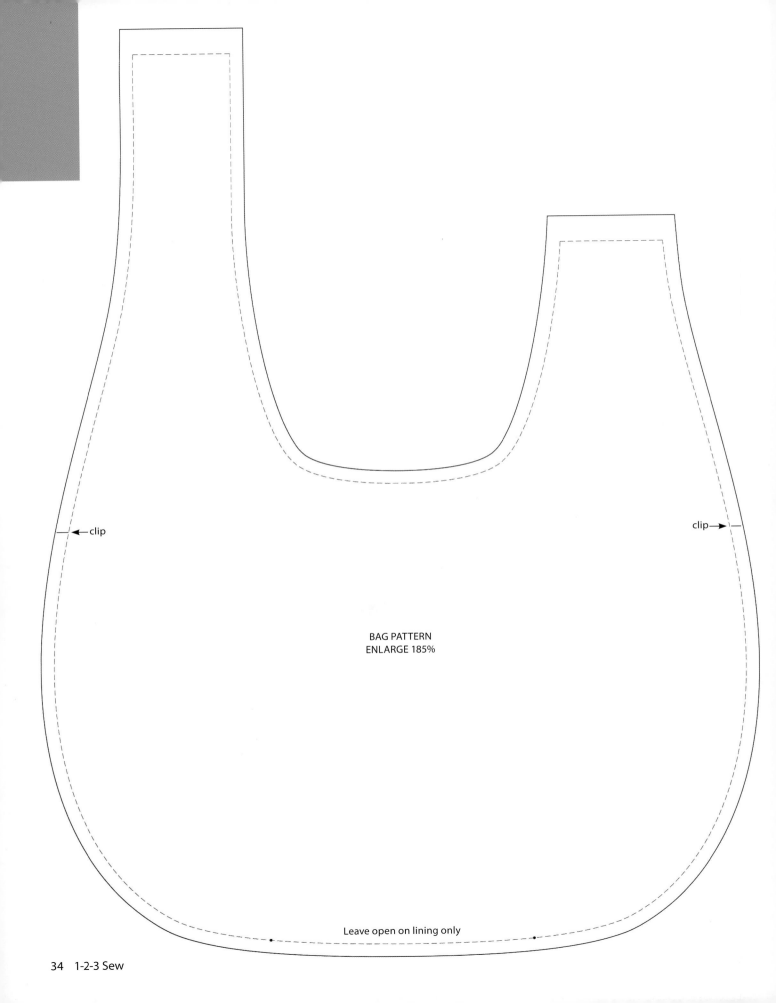

BAG PATTERN
ENLARGE 185%

clip

clip

Leave open on lining only

skirted styles

Give a plain round table a face-lift with a long covering that's a cinch to make. It's so easy, you'll want to create several in your favorite fabrics and interchange them with the seasons—or whenever it strikes your fancy.

Photographed by Hopkins Associates and Jon Jensen

round table skirt
INSTRUCTIONS

1. Determine the cutting diameter of the table topper. Using a tape measure, measure the diameter of the tabletop. Then measure the drop from tabletop to floor; double this measurement and add the diameter. Add 1" for a narrow hem or add 2" for a wider hem.

2. Cut fabric width to cutting diameter found in Step 1. If cutting diameter of table topper is wider than the fabric, use ½" seams to join fabric pieces, long edges together and matching patterns if necessary, to create a larger topper piece. Sew fabric pieces together along sides of table skirt rather than down the center to make seams less noticeable *(Diagram 1, below)*. Press seams open.

MATERIALS

- Desired fabric for table skirt
- Desired fabric for square table topper (optional)
- Three-leg round decorator table
- Pencil or fabric marker
- String and straight pin
- Sharp fabric scissors
- Bullion fringe or other desired trim (optional)

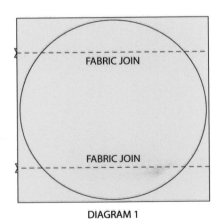

FABRIC JOIN

FABRIC JOIN

DIAGRAM 1

3. Fold topper piece in half, then in half again to make a square. The square measurement should be equal to the cutting diameter measurement found in Step 1.

4. Tie a string to a pencil or fabric marker and pin other end of the string to the folded corner of the topper piece. Adjust string's length to half the diameter of the table skirt. As if drawing an arc with a compass, swing fabric marker while keeping the string taut to mark a quarter circle on topper piece *(Diagram 2, above right)*.

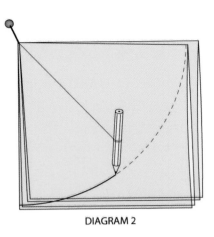

DIAGRAM 2

5. Using sharp fabric scissors, cut along the line through all layers of topper piece to make table skirt.

6. Hem curved edge of table skirt using either a narrow or wide hem as determined in Step 1.

To create a fringed edge, *shown opposite*, cut fringe using cutting diameter measurement found in Step 1. Pin fringe to hemmed table skirt edge so the bottom of the fringe is even with table skirt's hemmed edge; topstitch in place along trim's header to complete table skirt.

square table topper (optional)
INSTRUCTIONS

1. Determine the cutting measurements of the square table topper. Using a tape measure, measure diameter of the table. Then measure desired drop for the topper; double this measurement and add the diameter. Add 1¼" for a hem.

2. Cut fabric to the cutting measurement found in Step 1 to make square topper piece.

3. To miter the corners, press each raw edge of topper piece under ¼", then turn each edge under 1"; press. Open each pressed corner, leaving the ¼" folded edge intact. Trim across corner *(Diagram 3, opposite)*. Fold diagonal edge under ¼"; press.

DIAGRAM 3

4. Fold hems back in place, folding corners so they meet at a 45-degree angle *(Diagram 4 and Diagram 5, below)*. Pin mitered corners and hem straight edges around topper piece. Slip-stitch mitered corners in place to complete square table topper.

DIAGRAM 4

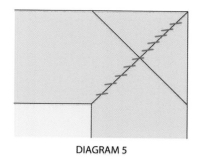

DIAGRAM 5

Give a basic table skirt a hint of formality by topstitching a length of long bullion fringe around the bottom hem. Instead of draping a square fabric topper on top, custom-fit a round piece of glass or mirror for an elegant and reflective touch.

window roll-ups

Hold up these shades with contrasting ribbon ties and let light flood into your room. When privacy is needed, untie the ribbons and let the shades unroll to cover the windows.

Photographed by Hopkins Associates

MATERIALS

- Plaid fabric (shade front)
- Eyelet (shade front)
- Plaid fabric (lining)
- Polka-dot grosgrain ribbon for ties
- 1"-diameter wooden dowel
- 1×1 mounting board
- Staple gun and staples
- Screwdriver and #8 wood screws

INSTRUCTIONS

All measurements include ½" seam allowances unless otherwise noted.

1. Determine the size to cut shade fabrics and lining. (Length = window length + 3½" for seam allowances and casing. Width = window width + 3" for seam allowances and outside window mount allowance.) Cut shade-front plaid and eyelet fabrics and plaid lining fabric to these measurements.

2. Layer plaid front piece and plaid lining pieces with right sides together and the eyelet piece in between the front and lining. Sew one short side and both long sides of the shade and lining together. Turn right side out; press. To form the casing, press bottom, raw edge under 1". Sew close to inner pressed edge.

3. Cut mounting board ½" shorter than the width of the sewn shade. Place shade, lining side down, on a flat surface. Position mounting board on lining side of the shade 2" below shade's raw edge *(Diagram 1)*. Fold raw edge side of the shade over the board. Staple through the fabric along back of the board *(Diagram 2)*. Insert dowel into casing sewn at the bottom edge as shown.

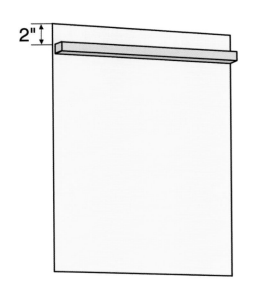

DIAGRAM I

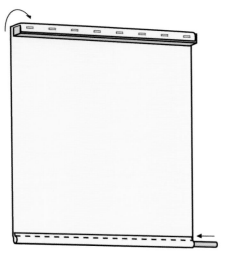

DIAGRAM 2

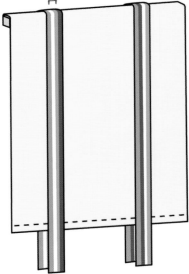

DIAGRAM 3

4. Determine the length to cut polka-dot grosgrain ribbon ties. (Length = window length × 2 + 18" for overhang.) Cut ribbon at calculated length.

5. Drape ribbon ties over top of board so that equal lengths hang on each side of shade

(Diagram 3, page 38). Position each tie as desired from side edges of the shade. Staple ties at the top of the board.

6. Attach shades to window using #8 wood screws.

take note

Reflect your style by using your favorite fabrics to make a handsome
and handy journal and portfolio ensemble.

Designed by Jennifer Paganelli of Sis Bloom   Photographed by Cameron Sadeghpour

journal cover
INSTRUCTIONS

From *each* cover print and flannel, cut:
- 1—14×29½" rectangle

From contrasting print (or cover print for matching tie) cut:
- 1—1½×42" strip for tie

1. With wrong sides together, layer cover print and flannel 14×29½" rectangles. Zigzag or serge together all edges to baste and finish edges.

2. Turn short edges of basted rectangles ¾" to the flannel side; topstitch close to edges to hem. With right sides inside, fold each hemmed edge 6½" toward the center to create a 14×15" rectangle. Sew 2" from each long edge (*Diagram 1, below*).

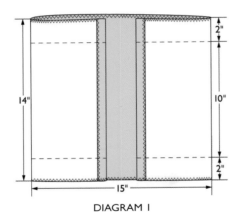

DIAGRAM 1

3. Turn under ends ¼" on print 1½×42" strip (*Diagram 2, below*). Then press strip in half lengthwise with wrong side inside. Open up fold and press under ¼" along long edges. Re-press strip along center fold; stitch close to both long edges to make the tie.

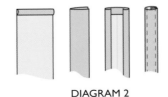

DIAGRAM 2

MATERIALS

- ½ yard *each* of print (journal cover) and white flannel (interlining)
- ⅛ yard contrasting print (journal cover tie, optional)
- ½ yard *each* of green print and pink stripe (portfolio cover and lining)
- 2⅛ yards ⅝"-wide grosgrain ribbon
- 4—1"-diameter O rings
- 7½x9¾" composition book
- Corrugated cardboard

finished journal cover: 7½×10"

finished portfolio: 12×20"

quantities are for 44/45"-wide, 100% cotton fabrics. All measurements include a ¼" seam allowance. Sew with right sides together unless otherwise stated.

4. To reduce bulk, trim upper layer only of top and bottom seam allowances (*Diagram 3, below*). Position tie as shown and topstitch in place to complete journal cover. Turn right side out and insert composition book (tie should be slightly to the front side of journal cover).

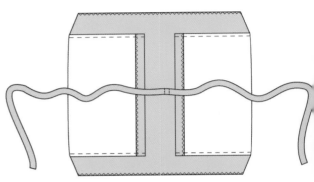

DIAGRAM 3

portfolio *(opposite)*
INSTRUCTIONS

From *each* green print and pink stripe, cut:
- 2—12½×20½" rectangles

From ribbon, cut:
- 2—38"-long ties, cutting ends at an angle to prevent fraying

From corrugated cardboard, cut:
- 2—12×20" rectangles

1. Sew together green print and pink stripe 12½×20½" rectangles along both long edges and one short edge. Turn right side out and press. Insert a cardboard rectangle and slip-stitch remaining edge closed to complete a portfolio half. Repeat to make a second portfolio half.

2. Loop one ribbon tie through two O rings; turn under ribbon end and hand-stitch in place, as shown in the illustration *below*. Repeat with second ribbon tie and remaining O rings. Wrap ribbon ties around portfolio halves, slipping free ribbon ends through both O rings, then back through just one O ring to secure.

O RING

optional project

Look for sturdy boxes to cover at local crafts stores, flea markets, and garage sales. Make a pattern for each box piece, adding enough extra fabric to allow for the fabric to wrap around the box edges. Spray the back of each fabric piece with spray adhesive, then wrap the fabric around the box like a gift, smoothing the fabric up along the sides and turning under raw edges where possible. For a softer box top, attach a piece of lightweight batting before covering it with fabric.

Use a portfolio (see the green version *above*) to tidy up your desk at night or to take important papers along with you. It's also great for toting scrapbook pages!

table topper

Practice your rotary cutting and straight stitching while creating a stylish, quilt-as-you-go table mat for the kitchen.

Designed by Kate Hardy   Photographed by Greg Scheidemann

MATERIALS

- ⅝ yard backing fabric
- ¼ yard *each* of eight assorted blue and green prints (table mat top)
- 18×22" piece (fat quarter) mottled brown (binding)
- 15×28" piece thin quilt batting
- Lightweight fusible web
- Pencil and straightedge
- Quilt basting spray (optional)

finished table mat: 13×26"

quantities are for 44/45"-wide, 100% cotton fabrics. All measurements include a ¼" seam allowance. Sew with right sides together unless otherwise stated.

CUT FABRICS

To make the best use of your fabrics, cut the pieces in the order that follows.

From backing fabric, cut:
- 1—15×28" rectangle

From *each* assorted blue and green print, cut:
- 3—1½×42" strips (you'll use 20 of the 24 strips cut)

From mottled brown, cut:
- Enough 2½"-wide bias strips to total 84" in length for binding *(For specific instructions, refer to steps 1 and 2 of "Piping Basics" on page 17.)*

ASSEMBLE AND QUILT TABLE MAT

1. Lay the backing fabric 15×28" rectangle on your work surface with the right side down. Place the thin quilt batting 15×28" rectangle on top. *Note:* If desired, use quilt basting spray to secure the layers together.

2. Using a pencil and a straightedge, draw a center positioning line through the center from one 28" edge to the opposite 28" edge.

3. With the right side up, place an assorted blue and green print 1½×42" strip across the middle of the layered background pieces; one edge should run along the center positioning line and the end should extend just beyond the top of the layered pieces. Trim the excess strip just beyond the bottom edge of the layered background pieces *(Diagram 1)*.

4. With the right side down, place a second assorted blue and green print 1½×42" strip atop the first strip; trim the excess strip as before. Sew together through all layers *(Diagram 1)*. Finger-press the top strip open.

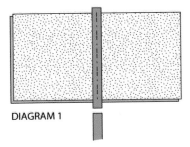

DIAGRAM 1

5. Continue adding assorted blue and green print strips in both directions until the layered background pieces are covered. Trim the layered pieces to a 13×26" rectangle *(Diagram 2)*.

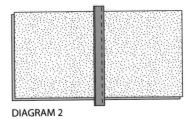

DIAGRAM 2

FINISH TABLE MAT

1. Using diagonal seams, sew together the mottled brown 2½"-wide bias strips to make an 84"-long strip. Use the strip to bind the table mat. *(For specific instructions, see "Bind It Right" on page 16.)*

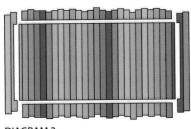

DIAGRAM 3

creature comforts

Treat your canine or feline friend to a cozy bed where they can catch a few zzzs. When it's time to clean it, just unzip the cover and toss it into the laundry.

Designed by Leah Anderson   Photographed by Cameron Sadeghpour

MATERIALS

- 12—18×22" pieces (fat quarters) assorted prints and plaids in red, teal, brown, white, and green (blocks, gusset)
- 1⅓ yards complementary print (bed cover back)
- 44"-round pet bed insert

pieced bed cover top: 41½" round

finished block: 10¼" square

finished bed cover: 44" round

quantities are for 44/45"-wide, 100% cotton fabrics. All measurements include a ¼" seam allowance. Sew with right sides together unless otherwise stated.

Circular pet bed inserts come in a variety of sizes, so to customize the pattern to your insert, first measure the diameter of the insert. Add 1" for seam allowances and make a circle pattern to this size. Assemble and join enough hourglass blocks and solid squares to equal the circle pattern; cut out the pattern.

These instructions are for a 44"-round pet bed insert.

CUT FABRICS

To make the best use of your fabrics, cut pieces in the following order.

Using a large piece of Kraft paper, wrapping paper, or pieces of printer paper taped together, trace around the pet bed insert to make the circle pattern; cut out the pattern.

From 8 assorted prints and plaids, cut:
- 8—11½" squares, cutting each diagonally twice in an X for 32 triangles total

From 4 assorted prints and plaids, cut:
- 8—10¾" squares

From scraps of assorted prints and plaids, cut:
- 51—3¼×5½" rectangles for gusset

ASSEMBLE HOURGLASS BLOCKS

1. Sew together two non-matching assorted print or plaid triangles to make a triangle pair (*Diagram 1*). Press seam in one direction. Repeat with remaining triangles for 16 triangle pairs total; press seam in same direction each time.

2. Sew together two triangle pairs to make an hourglass block (*Diagram 2*). Press seam in one direction. The block should be 10¾" square including seam allowances. Repeat to make 8 hourglass blocks total.

DIAGRAM 1   DIAGRAM 2

ASSEMBLE BED COVER

1. Referring to the Quilt Assembly Diagram *opposite*, lay out the hourglass blocks and 8 assorted print and plaid 10¾" squares in four horizontal rows.

2. Sew together blocks in each row. Press seams toward the 10¾" squares. Join rows to make the bed-cover top. Press seams in one direction. The pieced bed-cover top should be 41½" square including seam allowances.

CUT OUT BED-COVER TOP AND BACK

With right sides together, layer the pieced bed-cover top and backing fabric. Lay the circle pattern on top of the layers and cut out a circle through all the layers.

ADD GUSSET AND ASSEMBLE

1. Referring to photo *opposite*, join 51 assorted print and plaid 3¼×5½" rectangles to make a pieced gusset strip. Press seams in one direction.

what is a fat quarter?

A fat quarter is a ¼ yard of fabric cut in a different shape than the traditional ¼-yard piece of 44/45"-wide fabric. While a traditional ¼-yard cut is narrow and long (9×44"), a fat quarter is nearly square (18×22"). Many quilters like the cutting options offered by a fat quarter. To get a fat quarter, a ½-yard fabric piece is cut in half crosswise, making two "fat" quarter yards. Found in most quilt shops, fat quarters (and fat eighths, which measure 9×22") are sold individually or packaged in bundles of a specific fabric line or color palette.

2. Sew the pieced gusset strip to the pet bed circles with a ½" seam allowance, inserting a long zipper in the bottom seam to make the cover removable for washing. Press seams toward gusset.

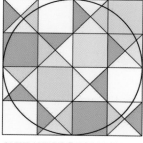

QUILT ASSEMBLY DIAGRAM

Better Homes and Gardens®
Creative Collection®

Editorial Director John Riha

Editor in Chief Deborah Gore Ohrn

Executive Editor Karman Wittry Hotchkiss

Managing Editor Kathleen Armentrout

Contributing Editorial Manager Heidi Palkovic

Contributing Design Director Tracy DeVenney

Copy Chief Mary Heaton
Contributing Copy Editor Mary Helen Schiltz
Proofreader Joleen Ross
Administrative Assistant Lori Eggers

Publishing Group President
Jack Griffin

President and CEO Stephen M. Lacy

Chairman of the Board William T. Kerr

In Memoriam
E. T. Meredith III (1933–2003)